By Kelly McKesten & Joe McEvoy

The

ABCs

of

SWIMMING

Illustrated by Maddie Schwimmer

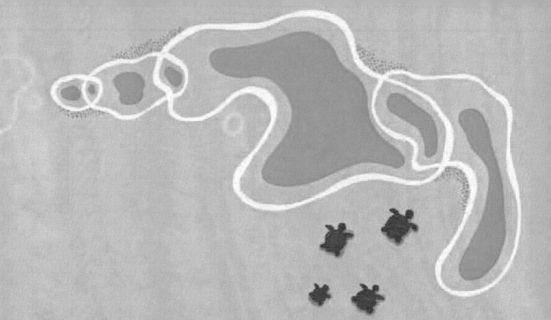

ISBN-13: 979-8-9859674-8-7

This publication contains the opinions and ideas of the authors. It is intended to provide helpful and informative material on the subject matter covered. It is sold with the understanding that the authors and publisher are not engaged in rendering professional advice in the book. The authors and publisher specifically disclaim any responsibility for any liability, loss, or risk, personal or otherwise, which is incurred as a consequence, directly or indirectly, of the use and application of any of the contents of this book.

www.theabcsofswimming.com

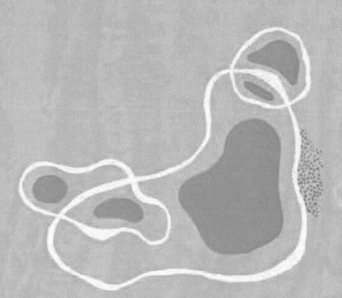

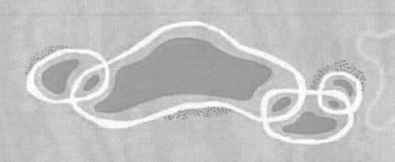

Dedication

For Jack and Sadie.
I love to watch you swim!
—Kelly

For my Mom,
My creative inspiration
—Maddie

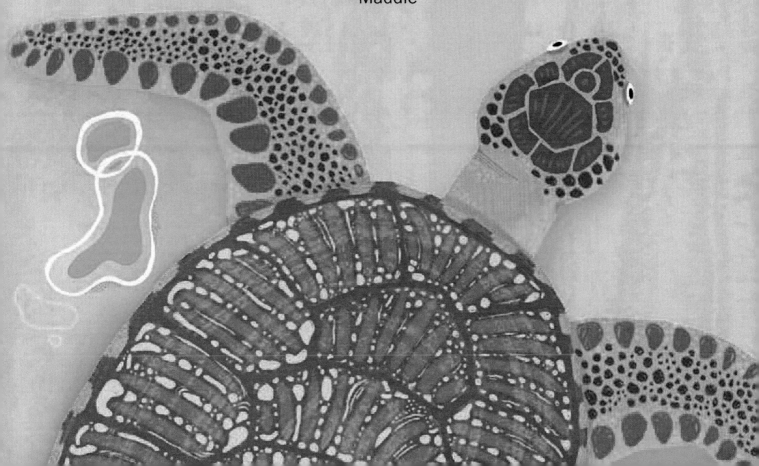

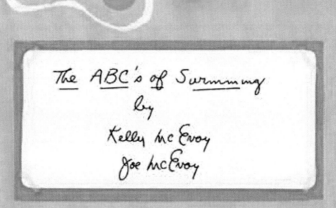

The ABC's of Swimming
by
Kelly McEvoy
Joe McEvoy

The Story Behind the Book

I started writing this book with my dad in 1993.

At the time, Joe McEvoy was a college swim coach and aquatics director, and he'd written two books about fitness swimming. I was a ten-year-old kid who loved to swim and draw. We started keeping a notebook with our ideas; he knew all the swimming terminology and I loved drawing pictures in the margins. When he died later that year, our notebook went into a box of keepsakes. I'd pull it out from time to time over the years and flip through the pages, always wishing we had been able to finish our book.

Now, thirty years later, I have two kids of my own who are learning to swim. Inspired by their love of the water, I reached back into that box for my dad's old notebook, and I finished writing our book. Then I was lucky enough to be introduced to Maddie Schwimmer, a talented artist who happens to be a swim coach, and who brought our story to life with beautiful illustrations.

My dad used to answer his phone by saying, "It's a great day to take a swim." My hope is that this book will help kids (and adults) find the same joy in swimming that he instilled in me, as well as his students and our family, all those years ago.

Kelly (McEvoy) McKesten

Aqua:

the water we swim in
and drink

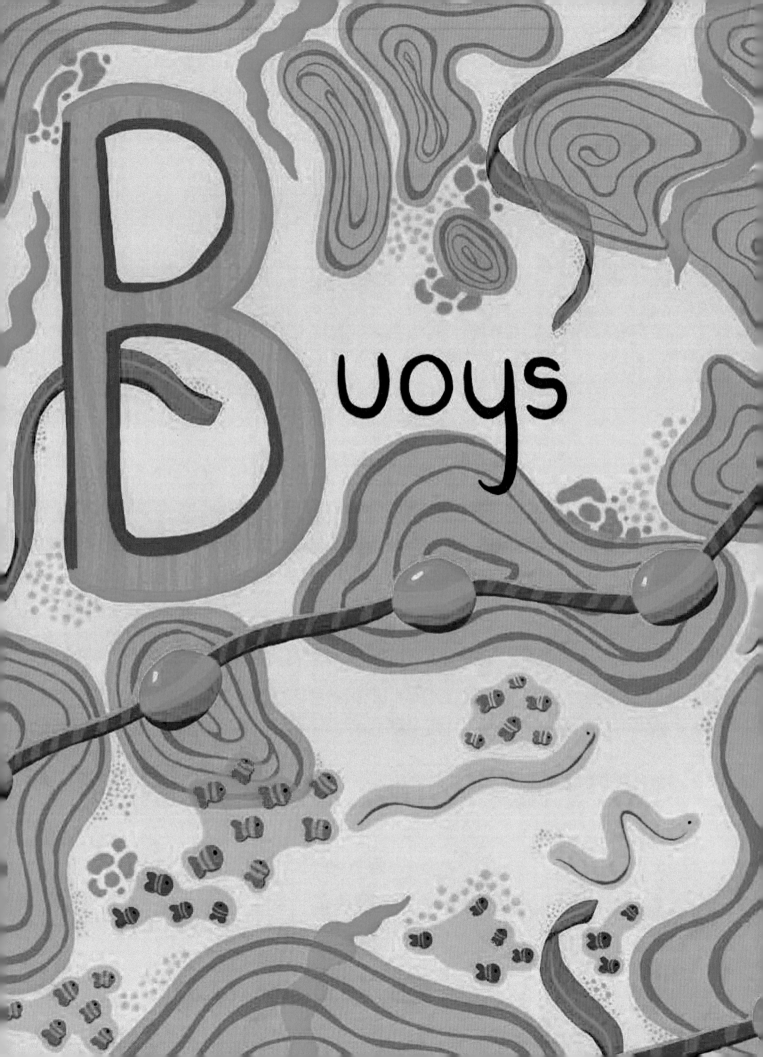

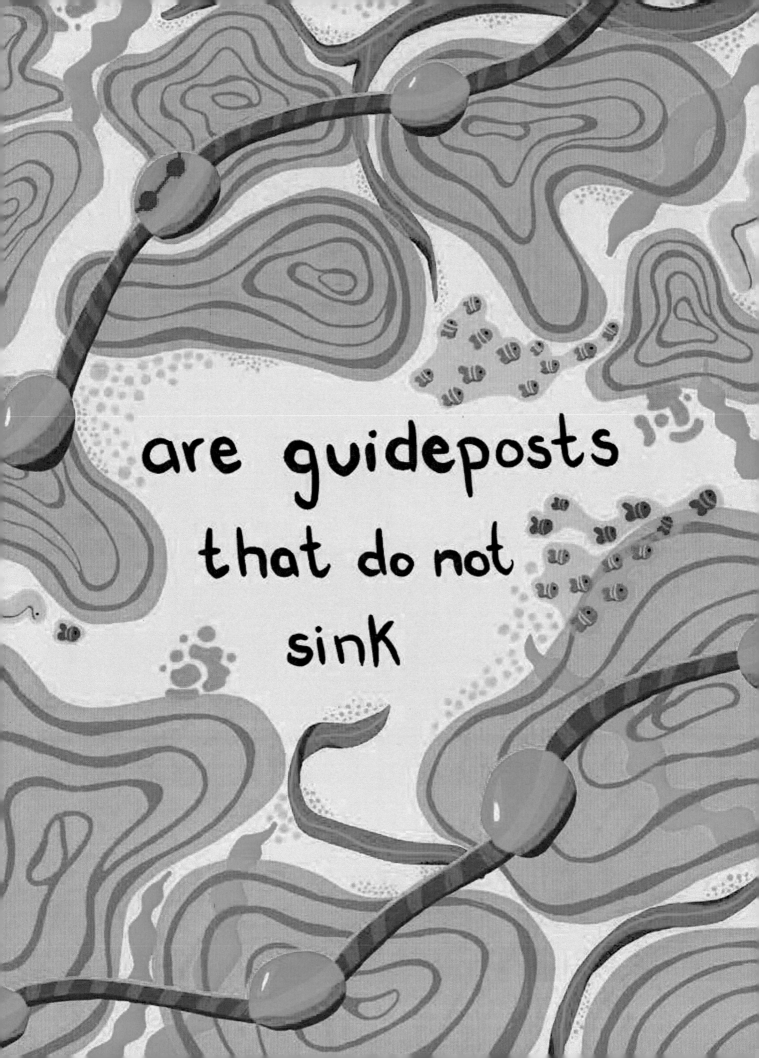

are guideposts
that do not
sink

Wear a

Cap

off the diving board;
fly through the air

Swimming is

Exercise

E for Everyone

Freestyling with

Flippers

is **F**ast

and it's **F**un

Goggles

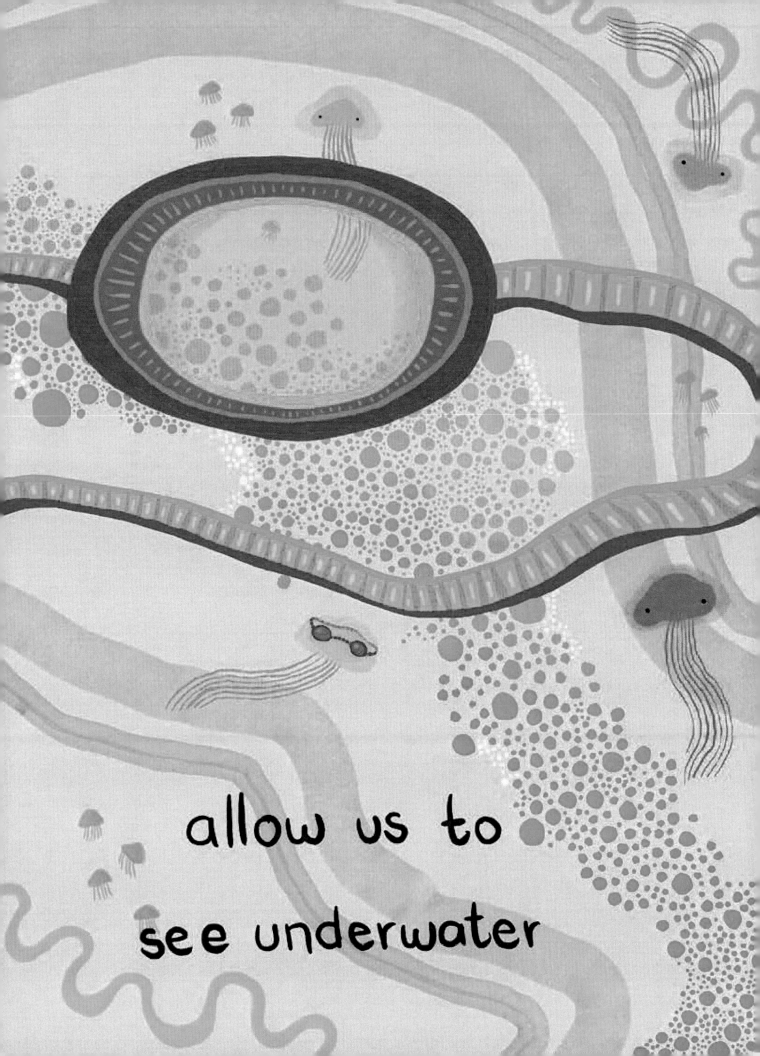

allow us to
see underwater

Hand paddles

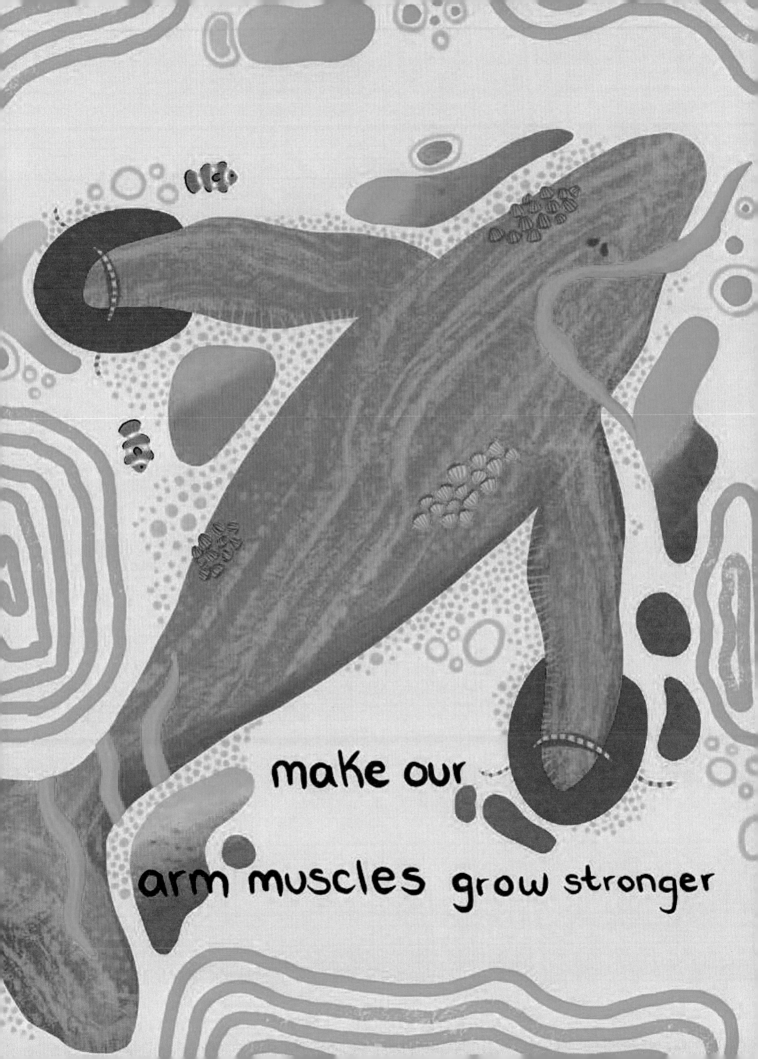

make our

arm muscles grow stronger

Individual medley:

Wear a life

Jacket

to keep you afloat

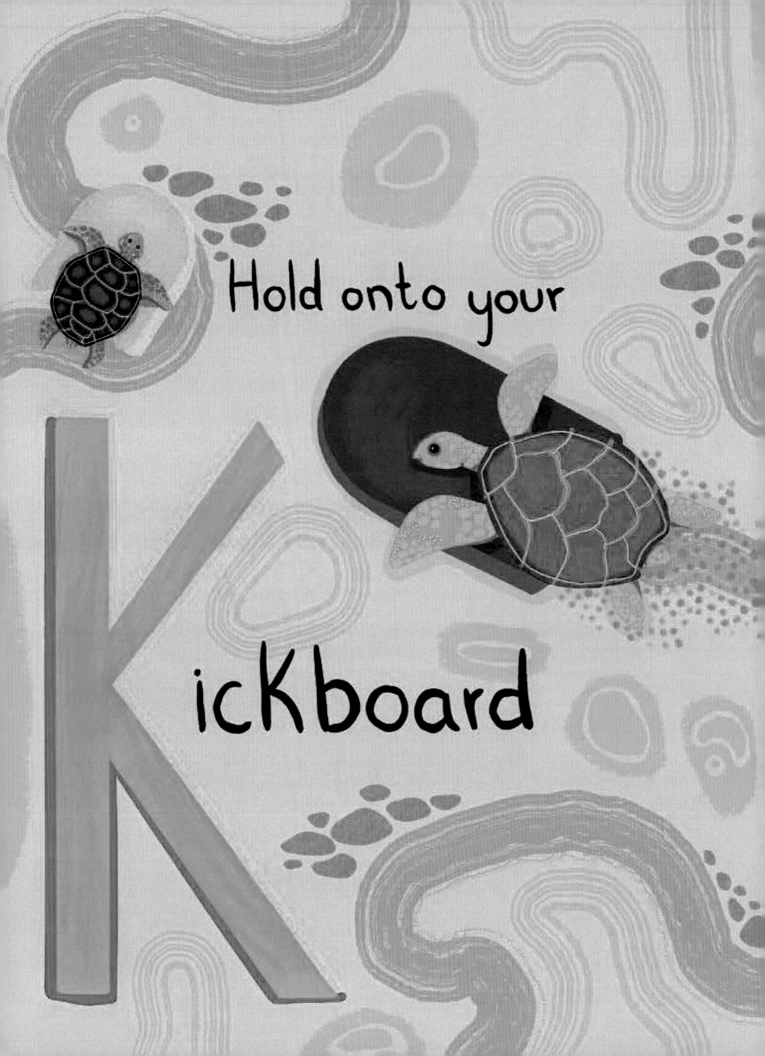

Hold onto your

Kickboard

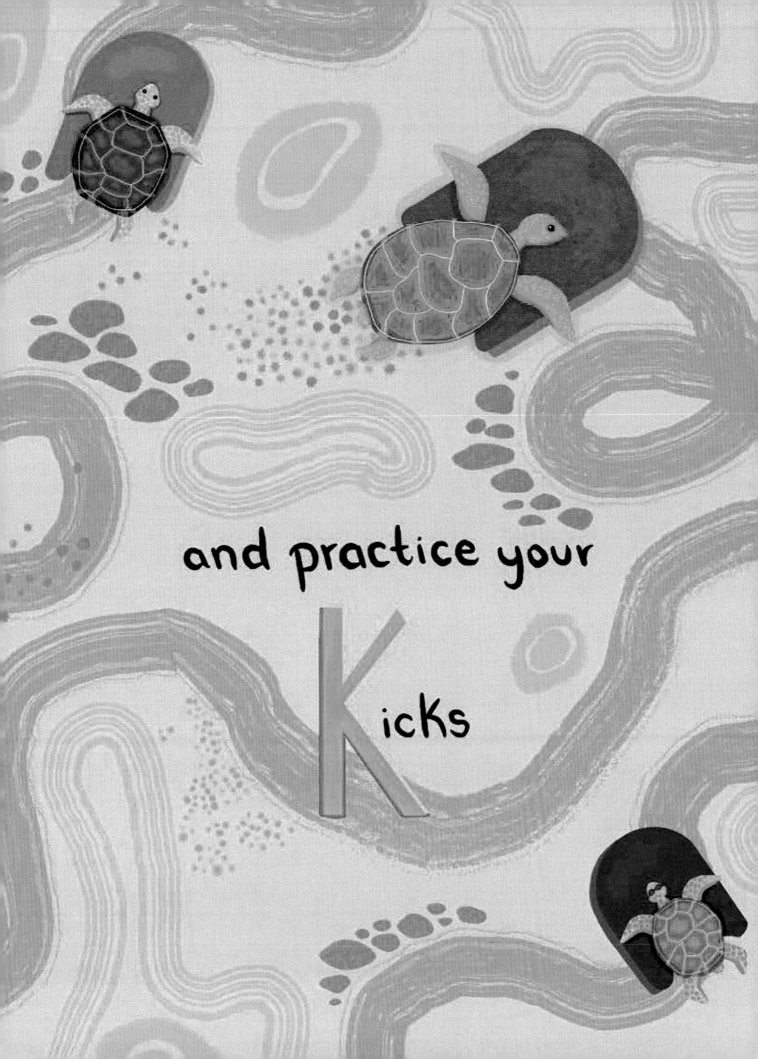

and practice your

Kicks

and stay in your Lane

while you work

on your flips

When teams

race each other

we call it a

Meet

In a

Natatorium

We swim in the Ocean

and splash in the waves

for swim **P**ractice

and **P**lay

It's always **Quiet**

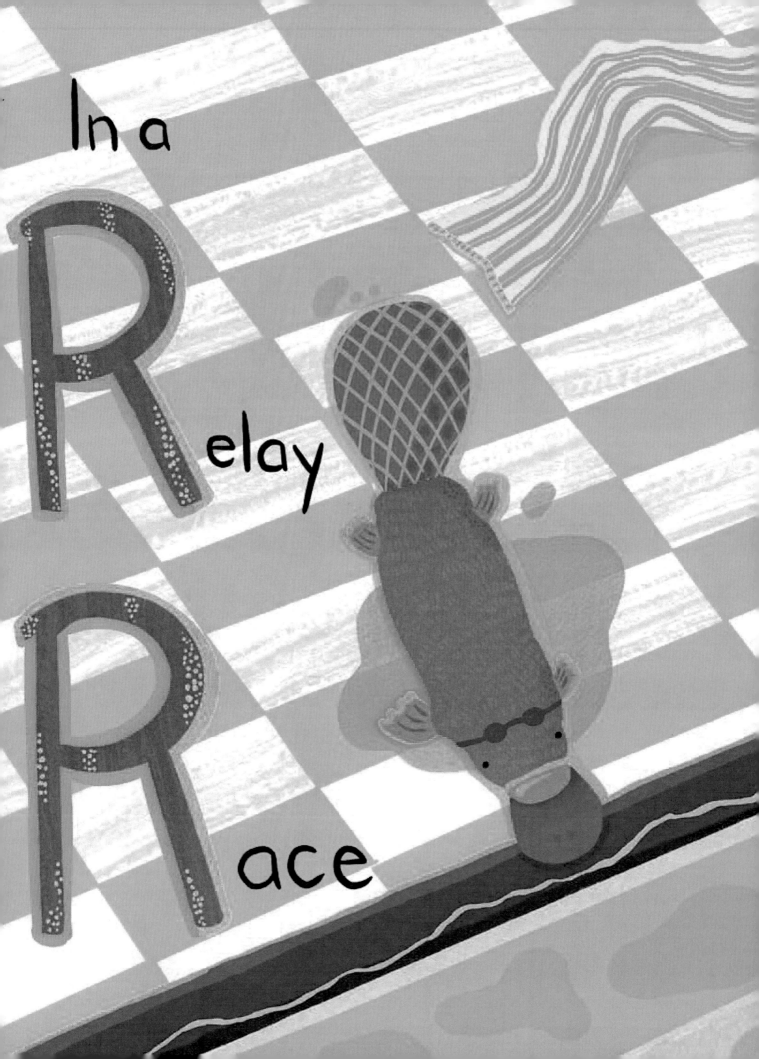

In a Relay Race

Synchronized Swimming is a

buoyant
ballet

Do a flip

Turn

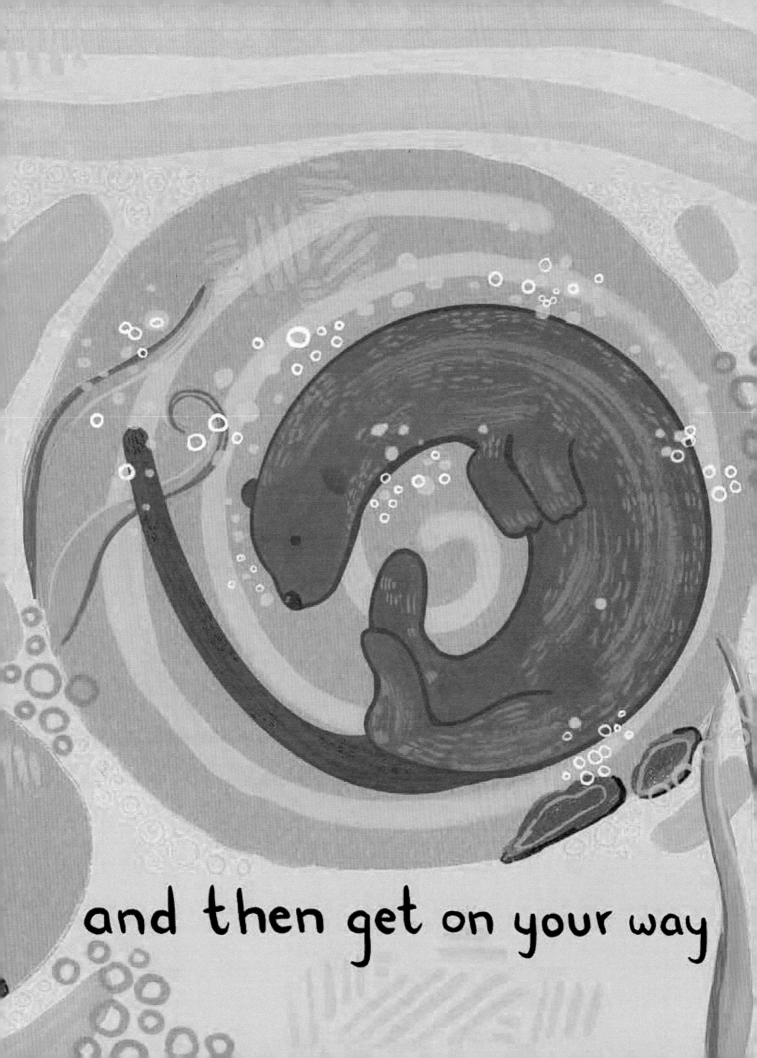

and then get on your way

Use
Underwater
ramps

Vacation?

Wait

for an adult
before taking a swim

to float

on your back

make an

X

with your limbs

Twenty five

Yards

is the length of

the pool

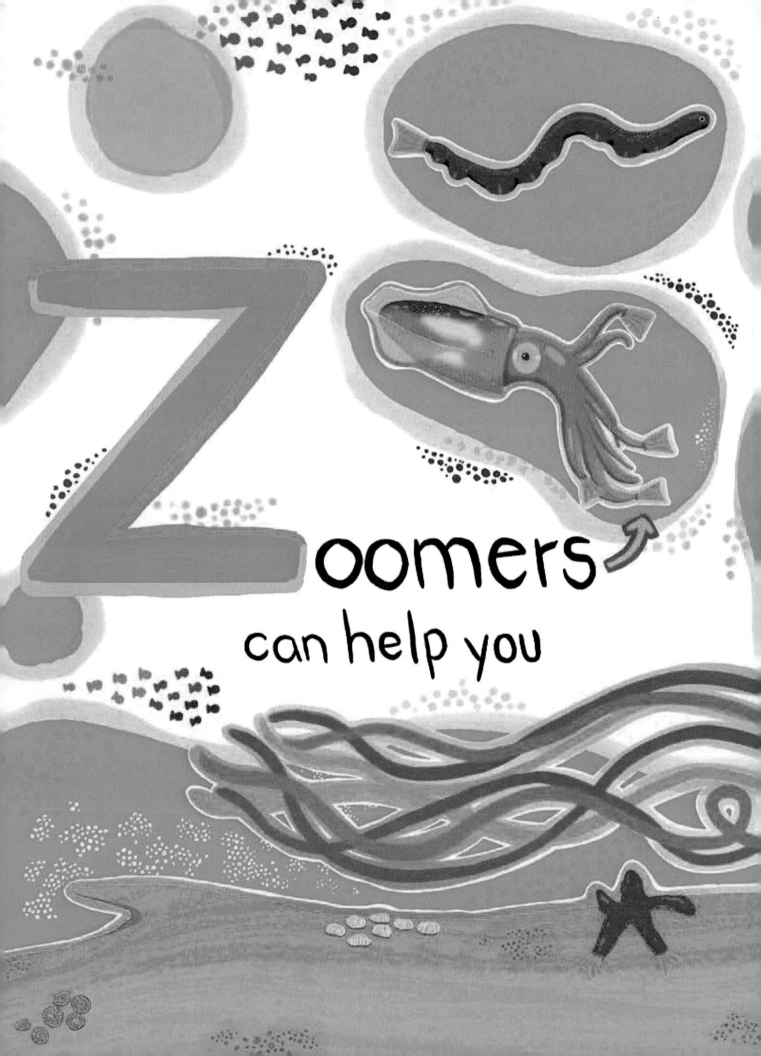

Zoomers can help you

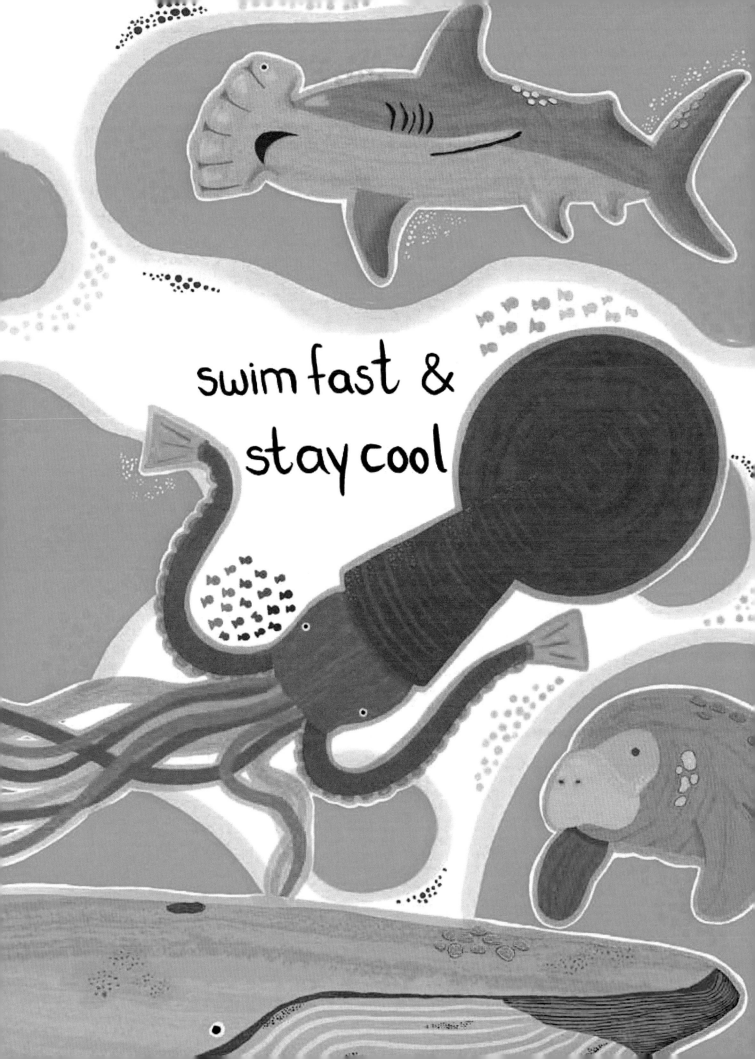

Acknowledgements

This book would not have been possible without the support and guidance of so many people over the last thirty years. First and foremost, I want to thank my mom, Pat McEvoy. You showed me that the best way to move through the grief of losing my dad was to do something kind for someone else. I'd also like to thank her husband, Mike Pasquarett, for being such a tremendous support to our family, and a wonderful grandfather to my children. Thank you to my brothers, TJ and Kevin McEvoy. Some of my most treasured memories are of swimming with you and our dad. Special thanks to the rest of my family and friends for their endless encouragement.

I'd like to thank my illustrator, Maddie Schwimmer, for being such a talented artist and delightful collaborator. You made the creative process an absolute pleasure. Huge thanks to our publisher, Thomas West, for not only believing in this story but for sagely guiding Maddie and me through the process of creating our first book. I'd also like to thank one of the earliest supporters of this book, Patrick Carrie, whose initial designs played a crucial role in the earliest stages of pitching this project. Tremendous thanks to my editor, Jessica Johnson, for helping to craft and elevate the words within these pages. Big thank you to Elizabeth Spiridakis Olson for her creative consultation.

I am thrilled to be working with the USA Swimming Foundation, which would not have been possible without the support of Elaine Calip. Thank you for believing in this book and for being such a lovely partner! Special thanks to Lyndsay Signor and Jennie Thompson for making the connection, and thank you to Tina Dessart for her thoughtful edits. Huge thanks to Nathan Adrian and Devin Ivester for their support.

Extra special thanks to my kids, Jack and Sadie, for helping me review pages from this book at bedtime. Their creative direction and feedback was essential in bringing this book to life. Enormous thanks to my husband, Jon, for being my biggest supporter and best friend. Finally, I want to thank my dad, Joe McEvoy. None of this would have ever been possible without him, and I'm endlessly grateful for every minute we had together.

The Creators

Kelly (McEvoy) McKesten is a lifelong swimmer and aquatics enthusiast. She can often be found swimming laps in her town's community pool, jumping over ocean waves, doing cannonballs off a diving board, sliding down a waterslide, soaking in a hot tub, jumping into a cold plunge, relaxing in a salt float, tubing across a lake, or meandering down a lazy river. *The ABCs Of Swimming* is her first book.

Joseph E. McEvoy believed that the swimming pool should be open like a library: from dawn until midnight, a place that wants you to swim in it. He earned his doctorate degree in physical education from Springfield College in Massachusetts. For more than twenty years he coached swimmers and divers of all ages and abilities, instilling in them the same infectious love for the sport that he had. He is also the author of *Fitness Swimming: Lifetime Programs* and *Swim Your Way to Fitness*.

Maddie Schwimmer started swimming on the local summer team at six years old and continued loving the sport throughout their collegiate swimming career. After graduation, they couldn't keep away from the pool and returned as a swim coach. They strive to keep the swimming pool an inclusive, diverse, and welcoming community space. Maddie is a self-taught artist and this is their first book.

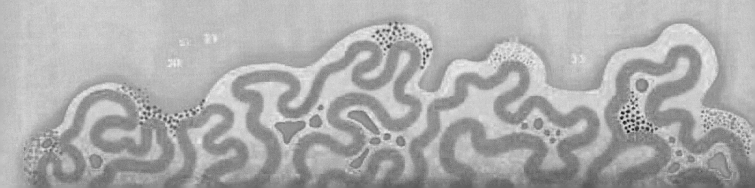

Swim Safety Tips

Always swim in a supervised area with a lifeguard on duty
and obey posted signs and flags.

Never swim or get into a body of water alone.

Stay within arms' reach of your swimming buddy or caregiver.

Children and inexperienced swimmers should wear
U.S. Coast Guard-approved life jackets.

Never use water wings or pool toys as life jackets.

If a fellow swimmer is in trouble, don't jump in to try to
help them. Instead, call for help. Stay on the side of the
pool and toss them an object like a ring buoy, or use a pole, oar, or
paddle to extend your reach.

Never swim during a storm or when there is lightning.

Apply sunscreen at least every two hours and
before and after swimming.

Learn to swim! You can find a swim lesson near you using
USA Swimming Foundation's QR code on the next page.

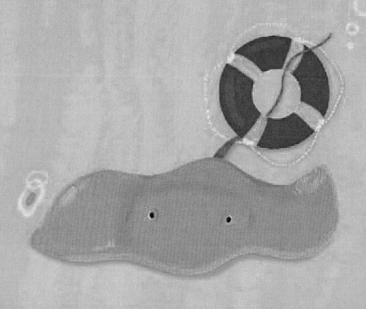

USA Swimming Foundation Swim Lesson Finder

Scan this code with your phone's camera to find a swim lesson near you!

Made in United States
North Haven, CT
17 June 2023